POKÉMON™

BEGINNER'S GUIDE

HOW TO TRAIN YOUR POKÉMON

CONTENTS

First published in Great Britain 2024 by Farshore
An imprint of HarperCollins*Publishers*
1 London Bridge Street, London SE1 9GF
www.farshore.co.uk

HarperCollins*Publishers*
Macken House, 39/40 Mayor Street Upper,
Dublin 1 D01 C9W8 Ireland

ISBN 978 0 00 861678 6
Printed in Italy
001

A CIP catalogue record for this title is available from the British Library.

Stay safe online. Farshore is not responsible for content hosted by third parties.

This book contains FSC™ certified paper and other controlled
sources to ensure responsible forest management.

For more information visit: www.harpercollins.co.uk/green

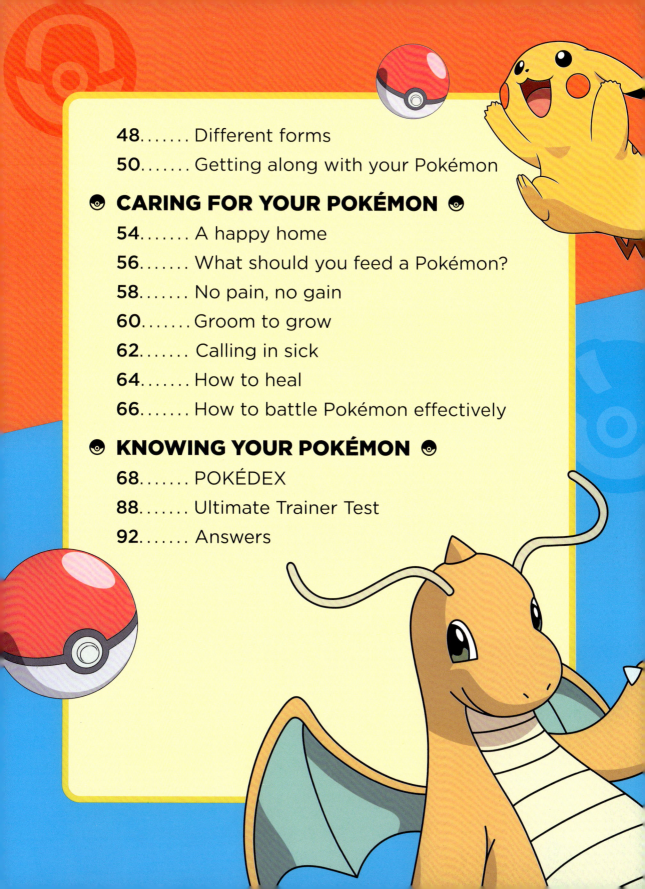

⚫ CARING FOR YOUR POKÉMON ⚫

⚫ KNOWING YOUR POKÉMON ⚫

INTRODUCTION

So, you want to catch your first Pokémon? What's next? This book will introduce you to the incredible world of Pokémon – you'll learn all the basics about what Pokémon are, where to find them and how to train and feed your Pokémon. Get ready to start your very own Pokémon adventure!

GETTING STARTED

WHAT IS A POKÉMON?

Pokémon are unique creatures. They all have their own special powers, abilities and personalities! Some Pokémon live in the wild, while others coexist peacefully in the human world.

Pikachu

Distinctive pointed ears

Pikachu's cheek pouches store electricity

Tail shaped like a lightning bolt

TRAINERS

The people who catch and coach Pokémon are called Trainers. They raise their Pokémon to be happy, healthy and to compete in friendly battles!

Squirtle

HELPFUL POKÉMON

Pokémon can use their skills to help humans with their jobs. For example, some Squirtle help fight fires with the Squirtle Firefighting Squad, and some Wigglytuff can help give medical aid in Pokémon Centres.

COME FIND US!

Pokémon have been found in these eight regions across the Pokémon world – from Kanto region to Galar region. Each region has a selection of three first partner Pokémon for Trainers to choose from, a Fire-type, a Grass-type and a Water-type Pokémon.

KANTO

Squirtle

Bulbasaur

Charmander

JOHTO

Totodile

Cyndaquil

Chikorita

HOENN

Treecko

Torchic

Mudkip

UNOVA

Tepig

Snivy

Oshawott

KALOS

Froakie

Chespin

Fennekin

SINNOH

Piplup

Turtwig

Chimchar

GALAR

Scorbunny

Grookey

Sobble

ALOLA

Popplio

Litten

Rowlet

POKÉMON ORIGINS

Most Pokémon hatch from Eggs! Waiting to find out which Pokémon your Egg will hatch into can be really exciting! Some Pokémon Eggs are looked after at Pokémon Day Care until they hatch.

Togepi

Togepi's shell is brightly decorated

TOP MARKS!

Pokémon Eggs have varying colours and identifying marks that hint at which Pokémon is inside. An Egg is ready to hatch once it begins to glow.

EGG-CELLENT WORK!

To help the Egg you receive from the Pokémon Day Care hatch, you should:

- Treat it with loving care.
- Polish it with a warm, soft cloth.
- Take it with you as you travel.

ASH'S EGGS

Famous Trainer Ash had a number of his Pokémon hatch from Eggs, such as Phanpy, Scraggy and Riolu.

Phanpy

Riolu

Scraggy

TRAINERS

Trainers raise, mentor and coach their Pokémon in friendship and battle! Skilled Trainers can also become Gym Leaders. They usually challenge opponents to Pokémon battles in Gyms – places such as big arenas or battling grounds – where they can fight and win official badges.

Goh

Ash

UNFRIENDLY COACHES

Not everyone is cut out to be a Pokémon Trainer. Occasionally, you will find Trainers, like Paul from Veilstone City in the Sinnoh region, who aren't very nice people. Paul treats his Pokémon unkindly and uses them just to win battles.

Paul

MEET ASH!

The most well-known Trainer is Ash Ketchum from the Kanto region. Ash began his Pokémon journey long ago and always works hard to train his Pokémon. Ash has a very strong relationship with his Pikachu.

BADGE OF HONOUR

After defeating a Gym Leader, you receive a badge. This proves to everyone that you won the Gym battle in that region.

GREAT FRIENDS

Trainers are not alone in the Pokémon world. There are various helpers who will guide Trainers on their journey. You might meet:

- Nurse Joy – she is an expert in healing Pokémon.
- Officer Jenny – she's the law! Jenny protects Pokémon and people from crime.
- Professors – there's one in every region. They know everything there is to know about Pokémon!

Professor Oak

Officer Jenny

Nurse Joy

USEFUL ADVICE

A Professor can help a Trainer by offering lots of useful advice. They can give technical data on Pokémon through a Pokédex and inform Trainers about the dangers they may find along their journey.

SPECIAL SKILLS

Coordinators and Connoisseurs have specialised knowledge about Pokémon. Connoisseurs, like Cilan from Unova region, have the difficult job of making sure a Pokémon and Trainer are perfectly matched. A Coordinator makes sure a Pokémon looks beautiful for contests and pageants.

Cilan

OTHER IMPORTANT HELPERS

Ash meets many new friends on his quest to become a Pokémon Master. They all have different skills and abilities such as:

- Brock – Pokémon Breeder and keen chef.
- Serena – talented Pokémon Performer.
- Solana – brave Pokémon Ranger.

EQUIP YOURSELF

Trainers need various tools and equipment to help them throughout their adventures. An essential tool for catching Pokémon is a Pokédex. This tool is an electronic encyclopedia of Pokémon facts and figures. It can:

- Tell you a Pokémon's height, weight and type.
- Help identify Pokémon habitats.
- Educate a Trainer about a Pokémon's needs.

Rotom Phone

POKÉDEX STYLES

Pokédexes change in appearance as technology improves. Professor Cerise gives Ash a smartphone that is possessed by a Rotom. This Rotom Phone has a Pokédex and a lot of new fun features!

TO THE MAX!

Dynamax is a phenomenon where a Pokémon grows to many times its normal size. Trainers can control this transformation by wearing a Dynamax Band. A few Pokémon species can even Gigantamax. These Pokémon become huge, have unique powers and often gain a different appearance.

Z-RINGS

Z-Rings are cool gadgets that contain Z-Crystals. They allow Trainers to access Z-Moves. These are very powerful moves that only certain Pokémon can carry out!

HAVING A BALL

Poké Balls are containers carried by Trainers to catch and carry Pokémon during their travels. They are thrown at opposing Pokémon in order to catch them. Some balls are better at catching Pokémon than others.
The steps are:

- Weaken a Pokémon by battling it with another Pokémon or using a potion.
- Throw a Poké Ball in the direction of the weakened Pokémon.
- Wait for the Poké Ball to rock back and forth and change from white back to its original colour.
- If successful, you have caught the Pokémon in the Poké Ball.

Standard Poké Ball

WEAKEN THEM FIRST

To catch a Pokémon you must first weaken it, you can do this by tiring it out in battle. However, some Pokémon are quite happy to be caught and don't put up much of a fight!

SPECIALITY BALLS

There are many types of Poké Balls, all with unique specialities. A Net Ball, for example, is great for catching Water-type and Bug-type Pokémon. A Beast Ball is perfect for capturing Ultra Beasts.

ALL THE POKÉ BALLS

Timer Ball

Great Ball

Repeat Ball

Quick Ball

Ultra Ball

Premier Ball

Master Ball

Net Ball

Dive Ball

Dusk Ball

Heal Ball

Luxury Ball

Nest Ball

Safari Ball

Poké Ball

TRAINER REQUIREMENTS

It takes hard work and dedication to be a Pokémon Trainer but the rewards are great. Here are some Trainer basics you need to know when getting started:

- Pick your first partner Pokémon wisely – you have a choice when you get your first Pokémon of Fire-type, Grass-type or Water-type. Choose carefully!
- Know your Pokémon – you will be spending a lot of time with them, so make sure to learn as much about them as possible!
- Learn to care for your Pokémon – Pokémon have lots of needs you should be aware of.

Dawn has travelled with Ash

Buizel

WHY TRAIN?

There are lots of reasons to become a Pokémon Trainer! Travelling the world with your Pokémon pal is great fun. Most importantly, being a Trainer teaches you all about teamwork, confidence and determination.

Pansage

Dwebble

THE JOURNEY BEGINS

From the age of ten, Trainers can begin their journey to catch and coach Pokémon. However, it is never too late to start learning and caring about Pokémon!

TRAIN YOUR OWN WAY

There isn't just one way to train your Pokémon. Some Trainers focus on battles, others on friendship and some even train their Pokémon to commit crimes!
However, all good Trainers share a bond with their Pokémon and care for them greatly.

ALL TYPES OF TRAINERS

There are many different types of Pokémon Trainers. Some like to specialise in just one type of Pokémon and become experts.

**Misty
Water-type**

**Iris
Dragon-type**

**Kiawe
Fire-type**

TEAM ROCKET

If there's trouble, it is usually the work of Team Rocket! Jessie and James work for crime boss Giovanni to capture Pokémon. These mischievous Trainers often clash with Ash and his friends.

Wobbuffet

Meowth

Jessie

James

TOUGH LOVE

Though Jessie and James use their Pokémon for wild schemes, they would never harm them. They show their love for their Pokémon by working closely as a team.

PICKING A POKÉMON

FINDING POKÉMON

You can find Pokémon everywhere across the known regions of the Pokémon world. Most Pokémon live in the wild. Here are some places to look:

- Trees – some Pokémon hang around on branches, so be sure to look up.
- Lakes and seas – many types of Pokémon live underwater and need to be caught on a fishing line.
- Forests and grassy fields – you might be lucky to find a Pokémon walking along a path.
- Caves – in the darkness, you might see Zubat or other cave-dwelling Pokémon.
- Big cities – some Pokémon like to hide in buildings like museums and shops.

Some Zubat live in deep, dark caves

Some Bulbasaur live in forests

WHY CATCH AT ALL?

A Trainer might want to catch a wild Pokémon to train them for future battles, evolve them or trade them with other Trainers. Sometimes Pokémon and their Trainers just bond for life, like Ash and Pikachu!

FINDING THEM IS THE EASY PART

Make sure you have the right tools available when you look for Pokémon. The right Poké Balls, fishing rods and enticing snacks can all help when searching for Pokémon.

GIFT AND TRADE

Not all Pokémon need to be caught. Sometimes you just feel a connection with a wild Pokémon and they choose to join your team! Others can be gifted by a professor when you enter a new region or obtained through using a Pokémon trading machine.

CREATING A POKÉMON TEAM

A Pokémon Trainer can collect and train as many Pokémon as they like. Great Trainers will try to catch lots of Pokémon to learn about how to raise them. Trainers quickly discover which Pokémon like to work in a team and which prefer to work alone.

Solo Wishiwashi join the school

Wishiwashi (School Form)

GREAT TEAMS

Some Pokémon prefer to have lots of company. This gives them a sense of community or safety. A solo Wishiwashi is very weak, but when they team up, they can change into a powerful school form. While wild Dragonite might like to live in a large group on Dragonite Island.

Prinplup

BETTER SOLO

A few Pokémon like to work alone. For example, Prinplup can be a little snooty and think they are better than the rest of their team. They prefer a solitary life to teamwork.

BATTLE BUDDIES

In battle, Pokémon Trainers can bring their best six Pokémon. Here are some top tips for choosing them:

- Pick the Pokémon you are most comfortable with.
- Try to match strengths against weaknesses.
- Remember to rest exhausted Pokémon!

JUST MY TYPE

Pokémon and their moves are categorised by these eighteen currently known types, with new types still being discovered! The most important thing is to create a Pokémon team with types that work for you.

NEW DISCOVERIES

The most recent type to be discovered was the Fairy-type. So far, it is known that Fairy-types are effective against Dragon-types. However, Fairy-types' power and abilities have yet to be fully understood.

Electric

Grass

Water

Dragon

Flying

Fighting

Steel

Bug

Rock

Ice

DUAL-TYPES

Pokémon can either belong to one type or two types, also known as a dual-type, where one of its types will be the primary type (I) and the other is the secondary type (II). The advantage of a Pokémon belonging to a single type will be fewer weaknesses against other Pokémon. A dual-type Pokémon will have more advantages. Which do you think would be better in a battle?

Starmie

Tentacruel

Dark

Ground

Normal

Psychic

Poison

Ghost

Fairy

Fire

BIG AND SMALL

Pokémon come in all shapes and sizes, from the tiny Alcremie to towering Corviknight. When battling and catching new Pokémon, remember it is easier to pit Pokémon of the same size against each other. Battling a very large Pokémon with a smaller one can be tricky, but it is not impossible!

Ash	Pikachu 1' 4" (0.4 m)	Alcremie 1' 0" (0.3 m)	Corviknight 7' 3" (2.2 m)	Drednaw 3' 3" (1 m

DOES SIZE MATTER?

Size isn't everything. An inexperienced Pokémon will have less stamina and skills than an experienced one. Also, Pokémon types are very important. For example, Water-type attacks have a stronger effect on Fire-type Pokémon. This could give a smaller Pokémon a chance to win!

BIG HEART

In the end, what matters most is the size of a Trainer and Pokémon's hearts. With courage, they can face any challenges!

	2.5 m
	2.0 m
	1.5 m
	1.0 m
	0.5 m
	0 m

Grookey 1' 0" (0.3 m) **Scorbunny** 1' 0" (0.3 m) **Sobble** 1' 0" (0.3 m) **Wooloo** 2' 0" (0.6 m) **Yamper** 1' 0" (0.3 m)

LIKE NIGHT AND DAY

When looking for a Pokémon, Trainers should remember that some prefer the dark of night, while others love a sunny day. Some have developed special skills, which help them thrive at their favourite time of day or night.

NIGHT SEEKERS

These Pokémon are most active at nighttime or in dark spaces. To adapt to the low light, Noivern hunts using special vibrations called ultrasonic waves, while Noctowl's eyes have developed to see clearly in even the murkiest light!

Noctowl

Noivern

Strong wings for flying in the night

SUNNY CREATURES

On a bright day, it is possible to find these Pokémon outside enjoying the warmth! Grass-types like Cherrim and Skiploom often love sunlight.

Solrock

Flower blooms only if it is over 18°C

Cherrim (Overcast Form)

Skiploom

Cherrim (Sunshine Form)

USE EVERYTHING YOU HAVE

Sometimes, you can wait day and night and still not find the Pokémon you are looking for. Try using lures, specialised Poké Balls and snacks to bait shy Pokémon.

TRICKY POKÉMON

New Trainers should be wary of selecting Pokémon with dangerous physical features or aggressive personalities. These fierce Pokémon can be hard to catch and even harder to train!

Cacnea

Thorny arms that can swing wildly

Toxapex

Toxic poison spikes

FIERCE FEATURES

While strength, spikes and poison can be helpful in battle, they can be dangerous to Trainers! There are a lot of Pokémon features that a Trainer should be wary of. For example, Toxapex and Cacnea have sharp spikes!

Liepard

DIFFICULT CREATURES

A Pokémon's personality is sometimes scarier than their spikes! Liepard can be moody and vicious, while Drednaw is highly aggressive!

Drednaw

DANGEROUS POKÉMON

These Pokémon also have qualities that can be a risk to their Trainers:

-  Basculin can have a violent nature.
- Bewear are very strong and can accidentally crush their friends in a hug.
- Vileplume shake out clouds of toxic pollen with every step.

Bewear

EVOLUTION

As your Pokémon grows in strength, it has the option to evolve! During Evolution, your Pokémon becomes more powerful and their name, size and sometimes type might change.

A Raichu evolves from a Pikachu

A Pichu evolves into a Pikachu

HOW TO EVOLVE

Most Evolutions occur by training Pokémon and using them in battle. After a certain amount of experience, the Pokémon can evolve. There are also certain stones that can bring on an Evolution.

Eevee (Normal)

Eevee Water (Vaporeon)

STAGES OF EVOLUTION

Most Pokémon Evolutions have three stages. For example, Pichu can evolve into Pikachu, then Raichu. However, some Pokémon, like Mew, don't evolve at all. Others like Munchlax evolve only once.

Munchlax

WHY NOT EVOLVE?

Why would you want Munchlax if Snorlax is more evolved? With first-stage Evolutions, Trainers can focus on different moves and skills. The Pokémon might also be happy the way it is and show no interest in evolving!

UNUSUAL EVOLUTIONS

Eevee is the Evolution Pokémon. It is unique because it can evolve into eight currently known Evolutions! But it can only evolve once.

Eevee Electric (Jolteon)

Eevee Fire (Flareon)

DIFFERENT FORMS

Evolution is not the only way Pokémon can change form. The appearance of some Pokémon can be affected by the environment they were raised in, the season or even their gender.

WHERE ARE YOU FROM?

Sometimes a Pokémon's colours and features show where in the world they come from. You can see this in:

- Shellos, who can be pink or blue depending on if they grew up in the cold East Sea or warm West Sea.
- Burmy, who cover themselves in materials from their local surroundings.
- Variant Pokémon from each region who look a little different to the regular versions.

Plant-covered Burmy

Sand-covered Burmy

Trash-covered Burmy

POKÉMON FOR ALL SEASONS

Sawsbuck change form throughout the year. Their fur can change colour, and the plants in their horns will bloom depending on if it's winter, spring, summer or autumn.

Winter

MALES AND FEMALES

Sometimes you can tell what gender a Pokémon is by its appearance. For example, female Meowstic have mainly white fur, while male Meowstic fur is mostly blue. These Pokémon might also have different personalities – female Meowstic are known for being a little less friendly than males.

Meowstic (Male Form)

Meowstic (Female Form)

Spring

Summer

Autumn

GETTING ALONG WITH YOUR POKÉMON

Now that you know how to catch, care for and train your Pokémon, how can you tell if the two of you are compatible – or even friends? It is very important that you and your Pokémon are on the same page before going out into the world!

COMMUNICATION IS KEY

Pokémon don't usually speak, so it can be hard to know what they're thinking. But in a few cases, it is possible to understand what a Pokémon is telling you:

- Some Pokémon can communicate telepathically with their minds, like Mewtwo.
- Yamask can speak through people who wear it as a mask.
- Team Rocket's Meowth speaks human and often acts as a translator for other Pokémon.

Charizard

FRENEMIES

Many Pokémon and Trainers have disagreements! Ash had trouble when his Charmeleon evolved into a stubborn Charizard – and even Pikachu can be a handful! The best thing to do is keep learning about your Pokémon. The more you know their personality, the better you will get along.

LET THEM REST

Pokémon Trainer Iris and her Emolga are a great team. Iris understands that Emolga likes to be cared for and rest in a Poké Ball. This helps them avoid fighting with each other!

Emolga

CARING FOR YOUR POKÉMON

A HAPPY HOME

Many Pokémon will make their home in a Poké Ball. This protects them while training and travelling. But you can't just throw your Pokémon inside a Poké Ball without thought! Make sure their environment is safe and stress-free by:

- Picking a Poké Ball that is best for catching that type of Pokémon.
- Keeping Pokémon healthy by taking them to a Pokémon Centre often.
- Letting your Pokémon battle in and visit their most comfortable areas (forests, seas, mountains and caves).

Combee

Combee love flowering fields

AREN'T ALL POKÉ BALLS THE SAME?

A comfortable home is important for happy, healthy Pokémon. Some types of Poké Balls are better at catching and keeping Pokémon. For instance, Pokémon caught in a Luxury Ball bond with their Trainer more quickly.

WHAT'S INSIDE A POKÉ BALL?

Unfortunately we don't know. The interior of a Poké Ball with a Pokémon inside it remains a mystery. What do you think it looks like inside?

FREE ROAMERS

Not all Pokémon will agree to live in a Poké Ball. Ash's Pikachu prefers to stay in the open by Ash's side!

WHAT SHOULD YOU FEED A POKÉMON?

A good diet is key when it comes to training a Pokémon. Most Pokémon enjoy foods such as Poké Puffs and berries. Some Pokémon need special diets, and their Trainers create meals just for them!

Tamato Berry

PICKY EATER

Try these tips and tricks if your Pokémon is fussy about their food:
- Be patient.
- Try giving it new foods.
- Develop your own recipes to offer your Pokémon.

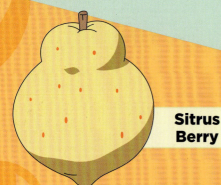

Sitrus Berry

Pecha Berry

Oran Berry

BERRY GOOD

Berries form a large part of a Pokémon's diet. There are many types of berries with different flavours and even special qualities.

YUMMY TREATS

Many Pokémon have a sweet tooth and love to eat sugary treats like macaroons and Poké Puffs, which can be found in the Kalos region.

NATURAL NIBBLES

Pokémon also enjoy tasty food found in the wild. Teddiursa loves to lick sweet honey off its paws. The honey is made from pollen collected by Beedrill.

Beedrill

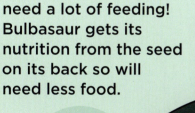

HUNGRY POKÉMON

Some Pokémon need to eat more than others. Snorlax likes to eat 360 kg of food every day so will need a lot of feeding! Bulbasaur gets its nutrition from the seed on its back so will need less food.

Snorlax

Belly full of food

NO PAIN, NO GAIN

Regular exercise is important for all living things to stay healthy. Some Pokémon enjoy physical activity more than others. In particular, Fighting-type Pokémon like to keep their bodies in tip-top shape!

Machop

Throh

CRUISIN' FOR A BRUISIN'

All Pokémon exercise differently. Throh and Sawk use martial arts as their go-to exercises. While Pokémon like Machop and Machamp like to do strength-training workouts.

Machamp

Sawk

BOUNCE IT OUT

Exercise doesn't need to be all about fighting and battling! A Popplio might work out by bouncing balloons on its nose.

Popplio

TRAINING FOR BATTLE

Some Trainers put their Pokémon through tough training to prepare them for battles. They might make their Pokémon lift heavy weights to improve their strength. Others might develop special exercise tools to train their Pokémon.

GROOM TO GROW

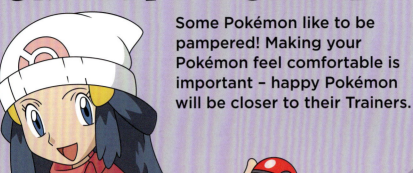

Some Pokémon like to be pampered! Making your Pokémon feel comfortable is important – happy Pokémon will be closer to their Trainers.

HAIR TODAY

Furfrou is known for being well-groomed and styled by its Trainers. There are even contests to determine which is the best-looking Poodle Pokémon.

Furfrou

Fluffy, white fur

DIY

Some Pokémon, like Litten, are low-maintenance and groom themselves. That's a load off your hairbrush!

Litten

FEATHERS OR SCALES?

Not all Pokémon can be groomed in the same way. Take Staravia and Magikarp. One has scales, while the other has feathers. Scaly Pokémon need a firm scrub brush, while feathered Pokémon like a much lighter, softer brush!

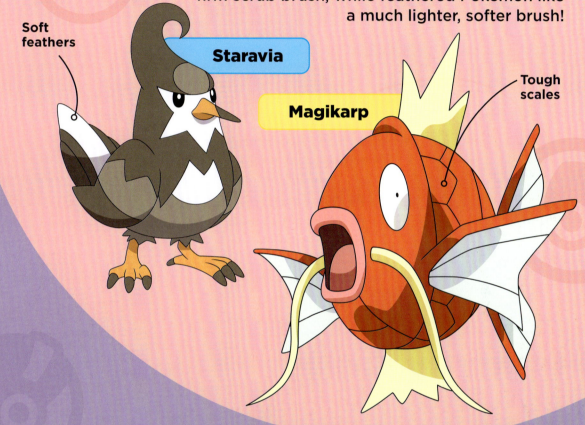

Soft feathers

Staravia

Magikarp

Tough scales

SPA BREAK

A day at the spa makes everyone feel relaxed! Grooming and attending soothing spas give Trainers and Pokémon a well-needed break.

Pokémon Paradise Springs Resort

CALLING IN SICK

There are a lot of reasons why a Pokémon might feel unwell. They may have an injury, be feeling weak after a battle, or just have a bad head cold! Some Pokémon will feel down if they see their Trainer is sad, too.

CHECKUP TIME!

When checking your Pokémon's health, remember to keep an eye on:

- Your Pokémon's colour.
- Your Pokémon's physical characteristics.
- Your Pokémon's mood.

HEALTHY SIGNS

Some Pokémon have features that tell you if they are healthy. A Charmander's tail-flame should always be bright and intense. If it starts to go out, that might mean that your Charmander is sick!

Bright burning flame

Charmander

SNOT AND TAIL SECRETIONS

When Cubchoo's drippy snot dries up, it might be feeling unwell. Equally, a change in the colour of Smeargle's tail secretion is also a sign that its mood may have worsened.

Happy green tail slime

Smeargle

Cubchoo

Healthy drippy snot

WHAT YOU CAN'T SEE

Keeping your Pokémon healthy with diet and exercise is only part of a Trainer's job. The better you get to know your Pokémon, the quicker you will be able to tell if something seems out of place.

HOW TO HEAL

What should you do if you notice that your Pokémon is sick? Luckily, there are a lot of medicines, remedies and places you can go to heal your exhausted or hurt Pokémon. Some options are:

- Take them to your nearest Pokémon Centre.
- Heal them with herbal remedies, medicine or berries.
- If you are in a battle, stop or switch out your Pokémon.

BE PREPARED

A good Trainer will always be prepared with healing berries and medicines while travelling with their Pokémon. Always try to stock up on healing salves and potions from the Poké Mart before long journeys or intense battles.

THE CENTRE OF ATTENTION

When a Pokémon is injured or unwell, head to a Pokémon Centre. They can be found in most towns and cities. The nurses in the Pokémon Centres are always named Nurse Joy. She and her Pokémon assistants will do their best to bring a Pokémon back to health.

Nurse's badge

Pocket for nurse supplies

Fluffy ears to listen to patients

Reassuring expression

Wigglytuff

DON'T BATTLE

An easy way to avoid injury is to be prepared to pull your Pokémon from battles and not use them again until they are fully healed.

HOW TO BATTLE POKÉMON EFFECTIVELY

Battling is a large part of a Pokémon's life and all Pokémon approach it differently. Battles can develop a Pokémon's confidence and skills. A good team will have Pokémon who enjoy battling and work well with others.

Primarina

WHY BATTLE?

Some Pokémon fight because they love the thrill of competition, while others are amazingly skilled at it. For Primarina, every battle is a stage, and this Pokémon loves to show off its dramatic battle moves.

MASTER OF ALL TYPES

It is a good idea to teach your Pokémon different types of moves. This will give them a strong chance against all types of attacks!

TYPE CAST

It is important to learn which types of Pokémon are strong or weak against other types. Pokémon trained in Fire-type moves, like Chimchar, might be weak against Water-type Pokémon. You can find all of this information in the Pokédex!

LEAD WELL

Pokémon and their Trainers are a close team. If you lack confidence and feel unsure, your Pokémon will, too! To turn you and your Pokémon into a battle-winning team, you'll need:

- A Pokémon's trust.
- A comfortable, well-rested Pokémon.
- Knowledge of Pokémon types and moves.
- Confidence in your Pokémon training.

KNOWING YOUR POKÉMON

THE POKÉDEX

Trainers need awesome research skills and as new Pokémon are discovered they should be logged on a Trainer's Rotom Phone. This Pokédex is where you will find important information about some of the Pokémon already discovered in the known world, from the Kanto region to the Galar region. Which one would you most love to catch and battle next?

ALCREMIE

FAIRY
0.3 m
0.5 kg

ABOUT:

When it trusts a Trainer, it will treat them to berries it's decorated with cream.

APPLETUN

GRASS · DRAGON
0.4 m
13.0 kg

ABOUT:

Its body is covered in sweet nectar, and the skin on its back is especially yummy. Children used to have it as a snack.

APPLIN

GRASS · DRAGON
0.2 m
0.5 kg

ABOUT:

It spends its entire life inside an apple. It hides from its natural enemies, bird Pokémon, by pretending it's just an apple and nothing more.

ARCANINE

FIRE
1.9 m
155.0 kg

ABOUT:

The sight of it running over 9978 km in a single day and night has captivated many people.

ARCTOVISH

WATER · ICE
2.0 m
175.0 kg

ABOUT:

Though it's able to capture prey by freezing its surroundings, this Pokémon has trouble eating the prey afterwards because its mouth is on top of its head.

ARCTOZOLT

ELECTRIC · ICE
2.3 m
150.0 kg

ABOUT:

This Pokémon lived on prehistoric seashores and was able to preserve food using the ice on its body. It went extinct because it moved so slowly.

ARROKUDA

WATER
0.5 m
1.0 kg

ABOUT:

If it sees any movement around it, this Pokémon charges for it straight away, leading with its sharply pointed jaw. It's very proud of that jaw.

BARRASKEWDA

WATER
1.3 m
30.0 kg

ABOUT:

This Pokémon has a jaw that's as sharp as a spear and as strong as steel. Apparently Barraskewda's flesh is surprisingly tasty, too.

BLASTOISE

WATER
1.6 m
85.5 kg

ABOUT:

Blastoise has water spouts that protrude from its shell. The spouts are very accurate and can shoot bullets of water with enough accuracy to strike empty cans from a distance of over 49 m.

BLIPBUG

BUG
0.4 m
8.0 kg

ABOUT:

Often found in gardens, this Pokémon has hairs on its body that it uses to assess its surroundings and check for danger.

BOLTUND

ELECTRIC
1.0 m
34.0 kg

ABOUT:

This Pokémon generates electricity and channels it into its legs to keep them strong. Boltund can run non-stop for three full days.

BULBASAUR

GRASS
0.7 m
6.9 kg

ABOUT:

Bulbasaur can be seen napping in bright sunlight. There is a seed on its back. By soaking up the sun's rays, the seed grows progressively larger.

BUTTERFREE

BUG · FLYING
1.1 m
32.0 kg

ABOUT:

In battle, it flaps its wings at great speed to release highly toxic dust into the air.

CARKOL

ROCK · FIRE
1.1 m
78.0 kg

ABOUT:

It forms coal inside its body. Coal dropped by this Pokémon once helped fuel the lives of people in the Galar region.

CENTISKORCH

FIRE · BUG
3.0 m
120.0 kg

ABOUT:

While its burning body is already dangerous on its own, this excessively hostile Pokémon also has large and very sharp fangs.

CHARIZARD

FIRE · FLYING
1.7 m
90.5 kg

ABOUT:

It spits fire that is hot enough to melt boulders. It may cause forest fires by blowing flames.

CHARJABUG

BUG · ELECTRIC
0.5 m
10.5 kg

ABOUT:

While its durable shell protects it from attacks, Charjabug strikes at enemies with jolts of electricity discharged from the tips of its jaws.

CHARMANDER

FIRE
0.6 m
8.5 kg

ABOUT:

It has a preference for hot things. When it rains, steam is said to spout from the tip of its tail.

CHARMELEON

FIRE
1.1 m
19.0 kg

ABOUT:

This Pokémon has a barbaric nature. In battle, it whips its fiery tail around and slashes away with sharp claws.

CHEWTLE

WATER
0.3 m
8.5 kg

ABOUT:

It starts off battles by attacking with its rock-hard horn, but as soon as the opponent flinches, this Pokémon bites down and never lets go.

CINDERACE

FIRE
1.4 m
33.0 kg

ABOUT:

It's skilled at both offence and defence, and it gets pumped up when cheered on. But if it starts showboating, it could put itself in a tough spot.

CLOBBOPUS

FIGHTING
0.6 m
4.0 kg

ABOUT:

Its tentacles tear off easily, but it isn't alarmed when that happens – it knows they'll grow back. It's about as smart as a three-year-old.

COALOSSAL

ROCK · FIRE
2.8 m
310.5 kg

ABOUT:

While it's engaged in battle, its mountain of coal will burn bright red, sending off sparks that scorch the surrounding area.

COPPERAJAH

STEEL
3.0 m
650.0 kg

ABOUT:

These Pokémon live in herds. Their trunks have incredible grip strength, strong enough to crush giant rocks into powder.

CORVIKNIGHT

FLYING · STEEL
2.2 m
75.0 kg

ABOUT:

With their great intellect and flying skills, these Pokémon very successfully act as the Galar region's airborne taxi service.

CORVISQUIRE

FLYING
0.8 m
16.0 kg

ABOUT:

Smart enough to use tools in battle, these Pokémon have been seen picking up rocks and flinging them or using ropes to wrap up enemies.

CRAMORANT

FLYING · WATER
0.8 m
18.0 kg

ABOUT:

This hungry Pokémon swallows Arrokuda whole. Occasionally, it makes a mistake and tries to swallow a Pokémon other than its preferred prey.

CUFANT

STEEL
1.2 m
100.0 kg

ABOUT:

If a job requires serious strength, this Pokémon will excel at it. Its copper body tarnishes in the rain, turning a vibrant green colour.

DOTTLER

BUG · PSYCHIC
0.4 m
19.5 kg

ABOUT:

It barely moves, but it's still alive. Hiding in its shell without food or water seems to have awakened its psychic powers.

DRACOVISH

WATER · DRAGON
2.3 m
215.0 kg

ABOUT:

Its mighty legs are capable of running at speeds exceeding 40 mph, but this Pokémon can't breathe unless it's underwater.

DRACOZOLT

ELECTRIC · DRAGON
1.8 m
190.0 kg

ABOUT:

This Pokémon's lower body is entirely too big when compared with its upper half. Powerful muscles in its tail generate electricity.

DRAGAPULT

DRAGON · GHOST
3.0 m
50.0 kg

ABOUT:

When it isn't battling, it keeps Dreepy in the holes on its horns. Once a fight starts, it launches the Dreepy like supersonic missiles.

DRAKLOAK

DRAGON · GHOST
1.4 m
11.0 kg

ABOUT:

It's capable of flying faster than 120 mph. It battles alongside Dreepy and dotes on them until they successfully evolve.

DREDNAW

WATER · ROCK
1.0 m
115.5 kg

ABOUT:

With jaws that can shear through steel rods, this highly aggressive Pokémon chomps down on its unfortunate prey.

DREEPY

DRAGON · GHOST
0.5 m
2.0 kg

ABOUT:

After being reborn as a ghost Pokémon, Dreepy wanders the areas it used to inhabit back when it was alive in prehistoric seas.

DRIZZILE

WATER
0.7 m
11.5 kg

ABOUT:

Highly intelligent, but also very lazy, it keeps enemies out of its territory by laying traps everywhere.

DUBWOOL

NORMAL
1.3 m
43.0 kg

ABOUT:

Weave a carpet from the springy wool of this Pokémon and you end up with something closer to a trampoline. You'll start to bounce the moment you set foot on it.

DURALUDON

STEEL · DRAGON
1.8 m
40.0 kg

ABOUT:

The special metal that composes its body is very light, so this Pokémon has considerable agility. It lives in caves because it dislikes the rain and rusts easily.

EEVEE

NORMAL
0.3 m
6.5 kg

ABOUT:

Thanks to its unstable genetic make-up, this special Pokémon conceals many different possible Evolutions.

EISCUE

ICE
1.4 m
89.0 kg

ABOUT:

This Pokémon keeps its heat-sensitive head cool with ice. It fishes for its food, dangling its single hair into the sea to lure in prey.

ELDEGOSS

GRASS
0.5 m
2.5 kg

ABOUT:

The cotton on the head of this Pokémon can be spun into a glossy, gorgeous yarn – a Galar-regional speciality.

ESPEON

PSYCHIC
0.9 m
26.5 kg

ABOUT:

It unleashes psychic power from the orb on its forehead. When its power is exhausted, the orb grows dull and dark.

ETERNATUS

POISON · DRAGON
20.0 m
950.0 kg

ABOUT:

The core on its chest absorbs energy emanating from the lands of the Galar region. This energy is what allows Eternatus to stay active.

FALINKS

FIGHTING
3.0 m
62.0 kg

ABOUT:

The six of them work together as one Pokémon. Teamwork is also their battle strategy, and they constantly change their formation as they fight.

GALARIAN FARFETCH'D

FIGHTING
0.8 m
42.0 kg

ABOUT:

The Farfetch'd of the Galar region are brave warriors, and they wield thick, tough leeks in battle.

FLAPPLE

GRASS · DRAGON
0.3 m
1.0 kg

ABOUT:

It flies on wings of apple skin and spits a powerful acid. It can also change its shape into that of an apple.

FLAREON

FIRE
0.9 m
25.0 kg

ABOUT:

It stores some of the air it inhales in its internal flame pouch, which heats it to almost 150 °C.

FROSMOTH

ICE · BUG
1.3 m
42.0 kg

ABOUT:

This Pokémon flies around with its huge, chill-emanating wings, causing a blizzard to chase offenders away. Clean meltwater is its favourite thing to drink.

GALVANTULA

BUG · ELECTRIC
0.8 m
14.3 kg

ABOUT:

It lays traps of electrified threads near the nests of bird Pokémon, aiming to snare chicks that are not yet good at flying.

GARCHOMP

DRAGON · GROUND
1.9 m
95.0 kg

ABOUT:

It flies at speeds equal to a jet fighter plane. It never allows its prey to escape.

GASTLY

GHOST · POISON
1.3 m
0.1 kg

ABOUT:

With its gas-like body, it can sneak into any place it desires. However, it can be blown away by the wind.

GENGAR

GHOST · POISON
1.5 m
40.5 kg

ABOUT:

Hiding in people's shadows at night time, this Pokémon absorbs their heat. The resulting chill causes the victims to shake.

GLACEON

ICE
0.8 m
25.9 kg

ABOUT:

Any who become captivated by the beauty of the snowfall that Glaceon creates will be frozen before they know it.

GOSSIFLEUR

GRASS
0.4 m
2.2 kg

ABOUT:

This Pokémon anchors itself in the ground with its single leg, then basks in bright sunshine. After absorbing enough sunlight, its petals spread as it blooms brilliantly.

GRAPPLOCT

FIGHTING
1.6 m
39.0 kg

ABOUT:

A body made up of nothing but muscle makes the grappling moves this Pokémon performs with its tentacles tremendously powerful.

GREEDENT

FIGHTING
0.6 m
6.0 kg

ABOUT:

If this Pokémon spots a berry tree it will immediately go and gather berries. It can chew through the toughest of berry shells.

GRENINJA

WATER · DARK
1.5 m
40.0 kg

ABOUT:

A Pokémon who can appear and vanish with a ninja's grace. It toys with its enemies using swift movements, while slicing them with throwing stars of sharpest water.

GRIMMSNARL

DARK · FAIRY
1.5 m
61 kg

ABOUT:

With the hair wrapped around its body helping to enhance its muscles, this Pokémon can overwhelm even Machamp.

GROOKEY

GRASS
0.3 m
5.0 kg

ABOUT:

It attacks with rapid beats of its stick. As it strikes with amazing speed, it gets more and more pumped.

GROWLITHE

FIRE
0.7 m
19.0 kg

ABOUT:

Extremely loyal, it will fearlessly bark at any opponent to protect its own Trainer from harm.

GRUBBIN

BUG
0.4 m
4.4 kg

ABOUT:

It uses its big jaws to dig nests into the forest floor, and it loves to feed on sweet tree sap.

GYARADOS

WATER · FLYING
6.5 m
235.0 kg

ABOUT:

Once it appears it goes on a rampage. Gyarados will remain enraged until it has destroyed everything around it.

HATENNA

PSYCHIC
0.4 m
3.4 kg

ABOUT:

If this Pokémon senses a strong emotion, it will run away as fast as it can. It prefers areas without people around.

HATTERENE

PSYCHIC · FAIRY
2.1 m
5.1 kg

ABOUT:

If you're too loud around it, you risk being torn apart by the claws on its tentacle. This Pokémon is also known as the Forest Witch.

HATTREM

PSYCHIC
0.6 m
4.8 kg

ABOUT:

To this Pokémon, strong emotions feel like loud noises. So it will pummel foes using the braids on its head to silence them. One blow would easily knock out a professional boxer.

HAUNTER

GHOST · POISON
1.6 m
0.1 kg

ABOUT:

In total darkness, where nothing is visible, Haunter lurks, silently stalking its next victim. Its touch causes endless suffering.

IMPIDIMP

DARK · FAIRY
0.4 m
5.5 kg

ABOUT:

This Pokémon sneaks into people's homes, stealing things and feasting on the negative energy of the frustrated occupants.

INDEEDEE

PSYCHIC · NORMAL
0.9 m
28.0 kg

ABOUT:

Through its horns, it can pick up on the emotions of creatures around it. Emotions that are positive are the source of its strength.

INTELEON

WATER
1.9 m
45.2 kg

ABOUT:

It has many hidden capabilities, such as fingertips that can shoot water and a membrane on its back that it can use to glide through the air.

IVYSAUR

GRASS · POISON
1.0 m
13.0 kg

ABOUT:

To support the weight of the bud on its back, Ivysaur's legs and trunk grow strong. If it starts spending more time lying in the sunlight, it's a sign that the bud will soon bloom.

JOLTEON

ELECTRIC
0.8 m
24.5 kg

ABOUT:

If it is angered or startled, it uses electricity to make the fur all over its body bristle like sharp needles that can launch and pierce foes.

JOLTIK

BUG · ELECTRIC
0.1 m
0.6 kg

ABOUT:

Joltik latch on to other Pokémon and suck out static electricity. They're often found sticking to Yamper's hindquarters.

KUBFU

FIGHTING
0.6 m
12.0 kg

ABOUT:

Kubfu trains hard to perfect its moves. The moves it masters will determine which form it takes when it evolves.

LEAFEON

GRASS
1.0 m
25.5 kg

ABOUT:

Galarians favour the distinctive aroma that drifts from this Pokémon's leaves. There's a popular perfume made using that scent.

GALARIAN LINOONE

DARK · NORMAL
0.5 m
32.5 kg

ABOUT:

It recklessly challenges opponents stronger than itself and uses its long tongue to taunt them. Once they are enraged, this Pokémon hurls itself at its foe, tackling them forcefully.

LUCARIO

FIGHTING · STEEL
1.2 m
54.0 kg

ABOUT:

It can tell what people are thinking. Only Trainers who have justice in their hearts can earn this Pokémon's trust.

LUDICOLO

WATER · GRASS
1.5 m
55.0 kg

ABOUT:

If it hears festive music, it begins moving in rhythm in order to amplify its power.

MAGIKARP

WATER
0.9 m
10.0 kg

ABOUT:

This underpowered Pokémon is easily pushed along strong river currents. It can occasionally jump high, but never more than two metres.

MEOWTH

NORMAL
0.4 m
4.2 kg

ABOUT:

It washes its face regularly to keep the coin on its forehead spotless. It doesn't get along with Galarian Meowth.

GALARIAN MEOWTH

STEEL
0.4 m
7.5 kg

ABOUT:

Living with a savage, seafaring people has toughened this Pokémon's body so much that parts of it have turned to iron.

MEW

PSYCHIC
0.4 m
4.0 kg

ABOUT:

Mew is said to possess the genetic composition of all Pokémon. It is capable of making itself invisible at will, so it entirely avoids notice even if it approaches people.

MEWTWO

PSYCHIC
2.0 m
122.0 kg

ABOUT:

A Pokémon created by genetic manipulation. But, even though humans created this Pokémon's body, they failed to endow Mewtwo with a compassionate heart.

MILCERY

FAIRY
0.2 m
0.3 kg

ABOUT:

This Pokémon was born from sweet-smelling particles in the air. Its body is made of cream.

MORGREM

DARK · FAIRY
0.8 m
12.5 kg

ABOUT:

With sly cunning, it tries to lure people into the woods. Some believe it to have the power to make crops grow.

MORPEKO

ELECTRIC · DARK
0.3 m
3.0 kg

ABOUT:

As it eats the seeds stored up in its pocket-like pouches, this Pokémon is not just satisfying its constant hunger. It's also generating electricity.

GALARIAN MR. MIME

ICE · PSYCHIC
1.4 m
56.8 kg

ABOUT:

It can radiate chilliness from the bottoms of its feet. It'll spend the whole day tap-dancing on a frozen floor.

MR. RIME

ICE · PSYCHIC
1.5 m
58.2 kg

ABOUT:

This Pokémon's amusing movements make it very popular. It releases its psychic power from the pattern on its belly.

NICKIT

DARK
0.6 m
8.9 kg

ABOUT:

Aided by the soft pads on its feet, it silently raids the food stores of other Pokémon. It survives off its ill-gotten gains.

NINETALES

FIRE
1.1 m
19.9 kg

ABOUT:

It is said to live for 1,000 years, and each of its tails is loaded with supernatural powers.

OBSTAGOON

DARK · NORMAL
1.6 m
46.0 kg

ABOUT:

It evolved after experiencing numerous fights. While crossing its arms, it lets out a shout that would make any opponent flinch.

ORBEETLE

BUG · PSYCHIC
0.4 m
40.8 kg

ABOUT:

It's famous for its high level of intelligence, and the large size of its brain is proof that it also possesses immense psychic power.

PERRSERKER

STEEL
0.8 m
28.0 kg

ABOUT:

What appears to be an iron helmet is actually hardened hair, while its claws have evolved into daggers. It lives for the thrill of battle.

PICHU

ELECTRIC
0.3 m
2.0 kg

ABOUT:

Despite its small size, it can zap even adult humans. It is unskilled at storing electric power and will discharge energy spontaneously.

PIKACHU

ELECTRIC
0.4 m
6.0 kg

ABOUT:

When Pikachu meet, they'll touch their tails together and exchange electricity through them as a form of greeting.

PINCURCHIN

ELECTRIC
0.3 m
1.0 kg

ABOUT:

It generates electricity when it digests food. It uses its five hard teeth to scrape seaweed off surfaces and eat it.

POLTEAGEIST

GHOST
0.2 m
0.4 kg

ABOUT:

Leaving leftover black tea unattended is asking for this Pokémon to come along and pour itself into it, turning the tea into a new Polteageist.

GALARIAN PONYTA

PSYCHIC
1.0 m
30.0 kg

ABOUT:

Its small horn hides a healing power. With a few rubs from this Pokémon's horn, any slight wound you have will be healed.

PSYDUCK

WATER
0.8 m
19.6 kg

ABOUT:

When it uses its mysterious power, it can't seem to recall having done so. It can't form any memories of these events because it goes into an altered state that is like a deep sleep.

RABOOT

FIRE
0.6 m
9.0 kg

ABOUT:

Its thick and fluffy fur protects it from the cold and enables it to use hotter fire moves.

RAICHU

ELECTRIC
0.8 m
30.0 kg

ABOUT:

Its long tail serves to ground this Pokémon, protecting itself from its high-voltage power.

GALARIAN RAPIDASH

PSYCHIC · FAIRY
1.7 m
80.0 kg

ABOUT:

Brave and prideful, this Pokémon dashes airily through the forest, its steps aided by the psychic power stored in the fur on its fetlocks.

RILLABOOM

GRASS
2.1 m
90.0 kg

ABOUT:

The Rillaboom with the best drumming techniques becomes the boss of the troop. It has a gentle disposition and values harmony among its group.

RIOLU

FIGHTING
0.7 m
20.2 kg

ABOUT:

It's exceedingly energetic, with enough stamina to keep running all through the night. Taking it for walks can be a challenging experience.

ROLYCOLY

ROCK
0.3 m
12.0 kg

ABOUT:

Most of its body has the same composition as coal. Fittingly, this Pokémon was first discovered in coal mines about 400 years ago.

ROOKIDEE

FLYING
0.2 m
1.8 kg

ABOUT:

It will bravely challenge any opponent, no matter how powerful. This Pokémon benefits from every battle – even a defeat increases its strength a bit.

RUNERIGUS

GROUND · GHOST
1.6 m
66.6 kg

ABOUT:

A powerful curse was woven into an ancient painting. After absorbing the spirit of a Yamask, the painting began to move.

SANDACONDA

GROUND
3.8 m
65.5 kg

ABOUT:

Its unique style of coiling allows it to blast sand out of its sand sac more efficiently.

SCORBUNNY

FIRE
0.3 m
4.5 kg

ABOUT:

A warm-up of running around gets fire energy coursing through this Pokémon's body. Once that happens, it's ready to fight at full power.

SILICOBRA

GROUND
2.2 m
7.6 kg

ABOUT:

Its large nostrils are specialised for spraying sand at its foes. While the enemy is blinded, it burrows into the ground to hide.

SINISTEA

GHOST
0.1 m
0.2 kg

ABOUT:

This Pokémon is said to have been born when a lonely spirit possessed a cold, leftover cup of tea. It is said to taste awful.

SIRFETCH'D

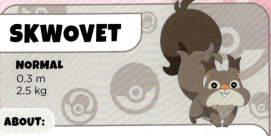

FIGHTING
0.8 m
117.0 kg

ABOUT:

Only Farfetch'd that have survived many battles can attain this evolution. When this Pokémon's leek finally withers, it will retire from combat.

SIZZLIPEDE

FIRE · BUG
0.7 m
1.0 kg

ABOUT:

It stores flammable gas in its body and uses it to generate heat. The yellow sections on its belly get particularly hot.

SKWOVET

NORMAL
0.3 m
2.5 kg

ABOUT:

Found throughout the Galar region, this Pokémon becomes uneasy if its cheeks are ever completely empty of berries.

SNOM

ICE · BUG
0.3 m
3.8 kg

ABOUT:

Within its internal organs, Snom amplifies the frigid air it gets from eating snow and then uses this cold air to create icicle-like spikes.

SNORLAX

NORMAL
2.1 m
460.0 kg

ABOUT:

This Pokémon's stomach is so strong, even eating mouldy or rotten food will not affect it.

SOBBLE

WATER
0.3 m
4.0 kg

ABOUT:

When scared, this Pokémon cries. Its tears pack the chemical punch of 100 onions, and attackers won't be able to resist weeping.

SQUIRTLE

WATER
0.5 m
9.0 kg

ABOUT:

The rounded shape and grooves on the surface of its shell help minimize resistance in water, enabling this Pokémon to swim at high speeds.

STONJOURNER

ROCK
2.5 m
520.0 kg

ABOUT:

It stands in grasslands, watching the sun's descent from zenith to horizon. This Pokémon has a talent for delivering dynamic kicks.

GALARIAN STUNFISK

GROUND · STEEL
0.7 m
20.5 kg

ABOUT:

Its conspicuous lips lure prey in as it lies in wait in the mud. When prey gets close, Stunfisk clamps its jagged steel fins down on them.

SYLVEON

FAIRY
1.0 m
23.5 kg

ABOUT:

There's a Galarian fairy tale that describes a beautiful Sylveon vanquishing a dreadful dragon Pokémon.

THIEVUL

DARK
1.2 m
19.9 kg

ABOUT:

It secretly marks potential targets with a scent. By following the scent, it stalks its targets and steals from them when they least expect it.

THWACKEY

GRASS
0.7 m
14.0 kg

ABOUT:

The faster a Thwackey can beat out a rhythm with its two sticks, the more respect it wins from its peers.

TOXEL

ELECTRIC · POISON
0.4 m
11.0 kg

ABOUT:

It has no problem drinking dirty water. An organ inside this Pokémon's body filters such water into a poison that is harmless to it. If you touch it, a tingling sensation follows.

TOXTRICITY

ELECTRIC · POISON
1.6 m
40.0 kg

ABOUT:

Capable of generating 15,000 volts of electricity, this Pokémon looks down on all that would challenge it.

UMBREON

DARK
1.0 m
27.0 kg

ABOUT:

On the night of a full moon, or when it gets excited, the ring patterns on its body glow yellow and it gains a mysterious power.

URSHIFU

FIGHTING · DARK
1.9 m
105.5 kg

ABOUT:

This form of Urshifu is a strong believer in the one-hit KO. Its strategy is to leap in close to its foes and land a devastating blow with a hardened fist.

VAPOREON

WATER
1.0 m
29.0 kg

ABOUT:

When Vaporeon's fins begin to vibrate, it is a sign that rain will come within a few hours.

VENUSAUR

GRASS · POISON
2.0 m
100.0 kg

ABOUT:

There is a large flower on Venusaur's back. The flower is said to take on vivid colours if it gets plenty of nutrition and sunlight. The flower's aroma soothes the emotions of people.

VULPIX

FIRE
0.6 m
9.9 kg

ABOUT:

While young, it has six gorgeous tails. When it grows, several new tails are sprouted.

WARTORTLE

WATER
1.0 m
22.5 kg

ABOUT:

Its large tail is covered with a rich, thick fur, which becomes increasingly deeper in colour as Wartortle ages. The scratches on its shell are evidence of its toughness as a battler.

GALARIAN WEEZING

POISON · FAIRY
3.0 m
16.0 kg

ABOUT:

This Pokémon consumes particles that contaminate the air. Instead of leaving droppings, it expels clean air.

WOBBUFFET

PSYCHIC
1.3 m
28.5 kg

ABOUT:

It hates light and shock. If attacked, it inflates its body to pump up its counterstrike.

WOOLOO

NORMAL
0.6 m
6.0 kg

ABOUT:

Its curly fleece is such an effective cushion that this Pokémon could fall off a cliff and stand right back up at the bottom, unharmed.

GALARIAN YAMASK

GROUND · GHOST
0.5 m
1.5 kg

ABOUT:

It's said that this Pokémon was formed when an ancient clay tablet with cursed engravings took possession of it.

YAMPER

ELECTRIC
0.3 m
13.5 kg

ABOUT:

This Pokémon is very popular as a herding dog in the Galar region. As it runs, it generates electricity from the base of its tail.

ZACIAN

FAIRY · STEEL
2.8 m
110.0 kg

ABOUT:

Able to cut down anything with a single strike, it became known as the Fairy King's Sword, and it inspired awe in friend and foe alike.

ZAMAZENTA

FIGHTING · STEEL
2.9 m
210.0 kg

ABOUT:

Its ability to deflect any attack led to it being known as the Fighting Master's Shield. It was feared and respected by all.

ZARUDE

DARK · GRASS
1.8 m
70.0 kg

ABOUT:

This Pokémon lives in a pack with others of its kind in dense forests. It's incredibly aggressive, and the other Pokémon of the forest fear it.

GALARIAN ZIGZAGOON

DARK · DRAGON
0.4 m
17.5 kg

ABOUT:

Thought to be the oldest form of Zigzagoon, it moves in zigzags and wreaks havoc upon its surroundings.

ZWEILOUS

DARK · DRAGON
1.4 m
50.0 kg

ABOUT:

Their two heads will fight each other over a single piece of food. Zweilous are covered in scars, even without battling others.

THE ULTIMATE TRAINER TEST

Are you fully prepared to enter the arena for your first Pokémon battle? Or are you in need of some more training time in the Pokémon Academy? Test your Pokémon knowledge with these tricky Trainer tests, each level is a little harder than the last.

TRAINER TIP: look back through this book if you get stuck.

BEGINNER — TRUE OR FALSE?

		TRUE	FALSE
1	Scorbunny is a Fire-type Pokémon.	○	○
2	There are eighteen known Pokémon types.	○	○
3	Ash Ketchum is originally from Hoenn.	○	○
4	Eevee has eight different evolutions.	○	○
5	First partner Pokémon are all Normal-type.	○	○
6	Ponyta has a Galarian form.	○	○
7	Rookidee is a Ghost-type.	○	○
8	All Pokémon can speak to their Trainers.	○	○
9	Frosmoth's favourite drink is pinap juice.	○	○
10	Jolteon is an Electric-type.	○	○

INTERMEDIATE CIRCLE YOUR ANSWER

1 Which of these **isn't** a Poké Ball?

> Net Ball **OR** Basket Ball

2 Rowlet is a first partner Pokémon in which region?

> Alola region **OR** Galar region

3 The Pokémon Centres are run by ...

> Nurse Joy **OR** Nurse Jenny

4 Grubbin is which single type?

> Grass-type **OR** Bug-type

5 How many tails does Vulpix have when it is young?

> Eight **OR** Six

6 Which Pokémon helps fight fires?

> Wigglytuff **OR** Squirtle

7 The Pokémon Staravia is covered in ...

> Feathers **OR** Scales

8 When you win a Gym battle, you get a ...

> Trophy **OR** Badge

9 What do Pikachu touch together when they first meet?

> Ears **OR** Tails

10 Snom is a dual-type, which two types is it?

> Ice and Bug **OR** Ice and Dark

MASTER

WRITE YOUR ANSWER

1 Which Pokémon is known for being styled by its Trainers.

2 Which Water-type Pokémon cries when it is scared?

3 What makes an Ivysaur's bud bloom?

4 The spirit of a Yamask is absorbed into which Pokémon?

5 Which Pokémon can generate 15,000 volts of electricity?

6 How many teeth does a Pincurchin have?

7 Which Dark- and Fairy-type Pokémon steals things?

8 Which Fighting-type Pokémon is made up of six Pokémon?

9 Why did Arctozolt go extinct?

10 Which Poké Ball helps a Trainer and a Pokémon to bond?

ADD UP YOUR CORRECT ANSWERS. HOW MANY DID YOU GET RIGHT?

WHAT YOUR POINTS MEAN

0-10 You are still at the beginning of your journey to becoming a Trainer, keep learning ... and battling!

11-20 Well done! Your knowledge of Pokémon is impressive. Stay on this path to fulfil your goals, Trainer!

21-30 Congratulations! You have risen to the challenge to become a Master Trainer!

ANSWERS

BEGINNERS

1. True
2. True
3. False
4. True
5. False
6. True
7. False
8. False
9. False
10. True

INTERMEDIATE

1. Basket Ball
2. Alola region
3. Nurse Joy
4. Bug-type
5. Six tails
6. Squirtle
7. Feathers
8. Badge
9. Their tails
10. Ice- and Bug-type

MASTER

1. Furfrou
2. Sobble
3. The sun
4. Runerigus
5. Toxtricity
6. Five teeth
7. Impidimp
8. Falinks
9. Because it moved so slowly
10. Luxury Ball